SUGGESTIONS FOR GROUP LEADERS

THE ROOM

Discourage people f[...] [...]in circle – all need to be equally involved.

. HOSPITALITY

Tea or coffee on arrival can be helpful at the first meeting. Perhaps at the end too, to encourage people to talk informally. Some groups might be more ambitious, taking it in turns to bring a dessert to start the evening (even in Lent, hospitality is OK!) with coffee at the end.

. THE START

If group members do not know each other well, some kind of 'icebreaker' might be helpful. You might invite people to share something quite secular (where they grew up, holidays, hobbies, significant object, etc.) or something more 'spiritual' (one thing I like and one thing I dislike about my church/denomination). Place a time limit on this.

. PREPARING THE GROUP

Take the group into your confidence, e.g. 'I've never done this before' or 'I've led lots of groups and each one has contained surprises'. Sharing vulnerability is designed to encourage all members to see the success of the group as their responsibility. Encourage those who know that they talk easily to ration their contributions. You might introduce a fun element by producing a bell which all must obey instantly. Encourage the reticent to speak at least once or twice – however briefly. Explain that there are no 'right' answers and that among friends it is fine to say things that you are not sure about – to express half-formed ideas. But of course, if individuals choose to say nothing, that is all right too.

. THE MATERIAL

Encourage members to read next week's chapter before the meeting, if possible. *There is no need to consider all the questions.* A lively exchange of views is what matters, so be selective. If you wish to spread a session over two or more meetings, that's fine.

You might decide to play all or part of the cassette at the end as well as the beginning. If you decide to use an extract, you are advised to use a different copy of the cassette from that used at the beginning. Get it ready at the precise point – finding a specific place can be difficult, especially when others are watching!

For some questions you might start with a few minutes silence to make jottings. Or you might ask members to talk in sub-groups of two or three, before sharing with the whole group.

. PREPARATION

Decide beforehand whether to distribute (or ask people to bring) paper, pencils, Bibles, hymn books etc. If possible, ask people in advance to read a passage or lead in prayer, so that they can prepare.

. TIMING

Try to start on time and make sure you stick fairly closely to your stated finishing time.

SESSION 1:
BRAVE NEW WORLD?

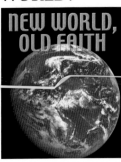

NEW WORLD, OLD FAITH

Eighteen months ago my mother celebrated her 90th birthday. As family and friends gathered, we reflected with admiration and astonishment on her life and times. She was born into a world without radio, TV or airports. The occasional car was a novelty. She told us of her amazement at meeting a black man, when she was seven. Doctors, teachers and policemen (they were all men) were highly regarded. The proverbial (and, we might add, dangerous) 'clip round the ear' was enough to control most young people.

Suing a hospital for failing to give appropriate treatment was unheard of. Family life was more or less stable – if not always happy. Divorce was rare, difficult and expensive. Two world wars would shake that stability, though no-one knew that then.

In my mother's childhood church attendance was high, though not universal. Uniformed movements for young people began to flourish and most of the nation's children attended Sunday School. Britain was a 'Christian country' which celebrated Empire Day. Non Christians were 'heathens'; the word was sung in hymns without embarrassment.

The term 'multi-cultural' had not been invented. The word 'environment' was seldom used and PC meant police constable and nothing else. Feminism was vigorous – though known by a different name – but few people dreamt of women priests. Almost every family had a bread-winner and he was male.

The idea of 'sex education' would have shocked most people. Child abuse was as widespread as it is now, but it was not openly discussed. At school there was no national curriculum and – the register apart – there was little paperwork for teachers. Later, schemes like National Savings, school milk and meals would be added. No one grumbled about the NHS because there wasn't one. There was no war against terrorism. The concept of 'world war' was about to be invented.

Church leaders felt secure. They were not always popular but they did count for something. Relationships between the churches were usually less cordial than they are today. Church was Church of England; chapel was everything else. Except for Catholics, that is. That church

Not so long ago, a Big Mac was a large raincoat and coke was for burning in your grate. Globalisation has changed all that and some commercial logos are better known that the Cross.

was coming to terms with the doctrine of Papal Infallibility, promulgated in 1870. Roman Catholics used Latin for the Mass and weren't allowed to pray with other Christians. There was little ecumenical activity. Councils of Churches were unthought of and 'Churches Together' would have seemed a strange concept.

Four generations gathered for my mother's 90th birthday party. The youngest family member was a few weeks old. Little Jonathan will grow up in a world where computer screens are as common as books. Or perhaps some new invention will replace both. It is highly likely that he will visit three or more continents but unlikely that he will stand on the moon. He will certainly be able to shop night or day, seven days a week. His brain will be bombarded with more facts in a month than his medieval forebears received in a lifetime. It is quite likely that he will live for over 100 years and he may need to travel north to escape the hot British summers. 'Gender balance' may become a problem as more and more parents choose the sex of their children.

It is indeed a new world which my mother and great-nephew now inhabit. And most people of my mother's generation have adapted to light-years of change with amazing skill and patience. But what about the 'old faith'? Has Christianity fared as well? How can the old faith engage effectively with the new world? Should it adapt and change in an attempt to fit in? Or should Christians consciously represent a counter-culture? And how can each of us play our part? These are some of the questions we will grapple with during these five sessions.

QUESTIONS FOR GROUPS

Please read page 1 (especially paragraphs 4 and 5) before the discussion starts. Some groups will not have time to consider more than a few questions. That is fine; this is not an obstacle course!

SUGGESTED BIBLE READING: Matthew 7:24-29

1. Raise any points from this booklet or the audio tape with which you strongly agree or disagree.

2. What are the most striking changes that have taken place in your lifetime? Do you regard these as positive or negative?

3. Read Romans 13:1-7. Doctors, teachers, policemen and politicians were held in high regard in the 'deferential society' of my mother's childhood. Is this true today? If not, why not? Does it matter?

4. Words can wound. Is political correctness a good thing - encouraging that sensitive, careful use of language which the Bible requires of us (James 3:1-12)? Or is it over-the-top and inhibiting? Which terms, if any, do you find offensive? Are we right to pass laws which inhibit free speech (e.g. against racism)?

5. Would you ever consider suing your doctor, hospital or school? In what circumstances? What are the causes and implications of our 'culture of litigation'?

6. The suffragettes won the vote for women. What change have modern feminists brought about – in church and society?

   (a) Do you welcome these changes?

   (b) Is there still a long way to go?

   (c) What effect has all this had upon modern men? Have they 'lost confidence', as is sometimes suggested?

7. Read Colossians 3:18-4:6

   (a) Bible teaching about male leadership was formulated in a very different world from ours. Should it and does it apply today?

   (b) What about the misuse of male power within the family? How should Church and State address this?

   (c) Can you think of female leaders in the Bible? What can we learn from them?

   (See Judges 4:4-10; Acts 16:11-15, and Acts 18:24-28)

8. 'Child abuse was widespread but not openly discussed.' Is this true? If so, modern openness is clearly a good thing. What other positive factors arise from the new world which we inhabit?

9. Are there positive features to be found in today's church going practices, in contrast to the practices of my mother's childhood?

10. Read Matthew 6:25-34

    (a) Is it harder to believe in God in today's new world than it was in my mother's childhood?

(b) How should church life and behaviour adapt to modern society? Should the churches exert a strong influence *against* some modern trends? If so, which and why?

In closing you might read 1 Corinthians 13 and pray for leaders of Church and State.

A new view of our old world.

SESSION 2:
ENVIRONMENT AND ETHICS

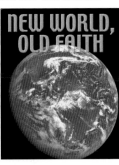

As a boy I walked in a London smog without realising that it was the cause of many deaths. When our house was declared to be in a newly created 'smokeless fuel zone' I felt resentment, for we were hard up and smokeless fuel cost more than coal. But smogs disappeared and I changed my mind.

For the first time I realised that we could influence our environment – for good or ill – by our attitudes and actions. Today every child knows this – and many care about it. The big question is: do they (and we) care deeply enough to make the radical changes in lifestyle which seem necessary for the survival of our planet?

Science and the resultant technology have given us a two-edged sword. The benefits are numerous. So are the hazards. We also realise that effective change is difficult and costly. We are beginning to understand that *not to* change will be even more costly – perhaps fatal.

We have the skills necessary for survival. But do we have the will? In the end, will we blow ourselves up, choke ourselves to death, or wreak havoc by self-induced climate change? Or will we heed the call of the Bible to be good stewards, implicit in the belief that 'in the beginning, God created the heavens and the earth (Genesis 1:1; see also Gensis 1:28)? Will we continue to regard the earth as a treasure chest to be ransacked or see it as a delicate network to be cherished and nurtured? Will we, as a poster on a teenager's wall challenges us, 'Take care of our local planet'?

This is a huge and urgent issue for our generation, but there are other, related, matters too.

- *The population explosion.* Rapid population expansion is still with us but the rate of growth is slowing down. Some European countries are declining in numbers. The slow-down in the developing world is due in large measure to the education of women. This tells us that aid, trade and debt remission are not acts of benevolence. They are in our own long-term self-interest. A thriving economy encourages education, health care and independence. And a healthy, more equal, world is likely to be a less violent world.

- *An ageing population.* In the so-called 'developing world' the average age is low. In the 'developed' world

In today's world, 100 million children live on the streets, with 10 million forced into prostitution. Some 13 million die of malnutrition each year and 2 million for lack of immunisation. Slavery or child labour claims another 150 million.

6

the population is ageing. As a result of good food, clean water and improved medical care, many in the West exceed the Bible's three score years and ten. As the decades roll by, I certainly welcome this! But it has huge and pressing implications for our society. In Britain there are more over-60s than under-16s. Pensions, family life, the housing stock, the length of working life and a host of related issues clamour for attention and solution.

- *Food.* Feeding the world's teeming millions should not be too difficult, for we produce more than enough food. Given modern irrigation and transportation, even countries subject to drought should not present an insoluble problem – until we put corrupt or inefficient governments, war, AIDS and greed into the equation. Advocates claim that genetically modified crops are the way forward. Opponents believe that this is a dangerous leap into the unknown. Oxfam posters touch our consciences and give the impression that 'they' depend on 'us'. But Britain imports a great deal of food. In reality we are dependent on the developing world for basics like tea, coffee and minerals.

- *Water.* Perhaps the single most urgent issue facing our world is the supply of clean water to all its citizens. Lack of this results in widespread disease and death. 'In the developing world contaminated food and water kill almost two million children a year' (*National Geographic,* May 2002). Yet universal clean water is a possibility, given the will and the resources. 'Am I my brother's keeper'? asks the Old Testament. The New Testament allows only one answer to this great question.

- *Medical technology.* Nearer to home we face complex issues which fill our newspapers and touch the lives of many. Abortion, assisted pregnancy, cloning, and the many questions to which they give rise, confront us daily in the media. To amplify just one: should children born by artificial insemination have the right to know the identity of their fathers? For most of us this is an interesting but distant question. For a growing number it is urgent and highly personal.

- *Euthanasia.* Advocates press for this with great energy and increased likelihood of success. Faced with a painful, terminal illness it seems an obvious way forward. But the unintended outcome of legalising 'mercy killing' might well be widespread misery. Many of the growing number of elderly people would face a huge additional pressure. Should they head for the Exit door, rather than become a 'burden' on family and friends? These and many other urgent issues cry out to be addressed and resolved.

QUESTIONS FOR GROUPS

SUGGESTED BIBLE READING: Genesis: 1:27-31

1. Raise any points from this booklet or the audio tape with which you strongly agree or disagree.

2. Some of the so-called 'developing' countries have become poorer over the past 20 years. Are terms like 'developing' and 'developed' an attempt to conceal this tough truth? Should we call a spade a spade in the interests of openness and fairness?

3. Read Amos 5:11-14. Imagine that you are on a ship with limited rations and many passengers. How would you feel if those nearest the kitchen received far more than others? Is that an accurate picture of life on earth, given the fact that a small proportion of the world's population (including us) use most of its resources? What can we do about it?

    (a) 'We want justice, not charity.' How should we respond to this cry from the world's poorest people?

    (b) Do you understand the phrase 'compassion fatigue'?

    (c) Does charity begin at home? Where does it end?

    (d) Do you recognise your dependence on the 'third world'?

4. 'To create a safer world you have to create a better world' (President George W. Bush, May 2002). Do poverty in the developing world and the misuse of power by the wealthy nations encourage terrorism, as some people maintain? If so, how should we conduct 'the war against terrorism'?

5. Do the Bible and Christian tradition throw light upon today's issues? Can ancient wisdom help solve modern problems? How? Discuss one or two of the big questions raised in this session e.g. GM crops, euthanasia, global warming, artificial insemination, unequal sharing of resources.

6. 'God has created a beautiful and resilient world for us to inhabit. He won't allow us to poison it but will come to our rescue.' Is this the voice of faith or of ignorance?

'It is a sobering thought that the early writings of the Jewish people (our Old Testament) encompass all the basic recommendations of world conservation strategy'.
(Professor David Bellamy)

7. 'Render to Caesar the things that are Caesar's.' Poor politicians! Most of them work very hard to address a raft of problems, with limited resources such as human intelligence and energy. Yet their judgements are vital for our survival. How can we encourage, challenge and support them? What is our role in relation to their work?

8. The Bible encourages good stewardship and *inter*-dependence – not *independence* (1 Corinthians 12:26-27). What does this mean in practice in today's complex world?

9. 'Why should I worry about posterity? What has posterity ever done for me?' (Groucho Marx). For the sake of the planet are you prepared to embrace changes in life-style, e.g. car rationing, unpackaged food, separating rubbish? What other changes might become necessary in the near future? How radical should we be?

In December 2002 scientists cracked the DNA code of the humble mouse. Mice and men have about 30,000 genes, with 80% in common. This has huge implications for medical research.

10. 'Honour your father and your mother' (Exodus 20:12).

   (a) How do you wish to be cared for in your old age?

   (b) If you were very ill, would you consider euthanasia?

   (c) If we legalised 'mercy killing' would this put pressure on old people, as suggested by Archbishop Rowan Williams on the tape, and Dame Cicely Saunders, founder of the hospice movement?

SESSION 3:

CHURCH AND FAMILY IN CRISIS?

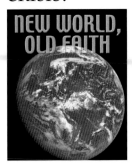

NEW WORLD, OLD FAITH

In 2002 I celebrated Easter twice. In March I was in Britain. In May I was in Greece, leading a group round famous Bible cities – Athens, Corinth, Philippi and Thessalonica. Our visit coincided with the Greek Orthodox 'Great Week' (our Holy Week) and Easter.

The churches were buzzing and overflowing. The worship was extremely traditional, though not formal and stuffy. The liturgy and music were ancient. The buildings were highly decorated with paintings and huge chandeliers; the priests wore colourful vestments; women did not appear in the sanctuary. I did not hear a single congregational hymn and I attended many services. There was a great deal of chanting by a small choir, together with incense, bustle, rapid crossing, kissing of icons, coming and going, and lighting of candles. I loved it all!

What a contrast to the churches in Britain with their congregational styles of worship and frequent innovations. Personally I welcome most of the changes which have occurred in my life-time. I enjoy the relaxed informality, the modern liturgies, the variety, many of the new songs and hymns and the ministry of women. Above all, I welcome the enhanced role of the laity. In the Church of England there are now more Readers (lay ministers) than paid clergy.

In the Roman Catholic Church, lay eucharistic ministers abound – male and female. All the churches would collapse without the commitment and energy of lay people. And, of course, it is lay people who fly the Christian flag in the workplace and marketplace.

A growing number of clergy have suffered the breakdown of a marriage. When I was at theological college an excellent fellow student (male of course) had to leave the course because his wife had left him. This seems extraordinary – and unjust – today. We accepted it as a sad necessity. All this points to another striking change in this 'brave new world'. Britain is the 'divorce capital' of Europe, with about one in three marriages ending in separation or divorce. This means, of course, that two out of three marriages hold together. That's the good news and perhaps it is remarkable given the pressures on modern marriage and family life.

Issues of gender and sexuality continue to rock the churches. The ordination of women in the 1990s did not

YORK COURSES LIST

December 2002

Courses for groups

- ### LIVE YOUR FAITH

  with Dr Donald English, Lord Tonypandy, Fiona and Roy Castle.

Tape + 1 booklet	£7.50
Extra booklets	£2.00 each

  SIX SESSIONS: *Jesus; Prayer; the Church; the Holy Spirit; the Bible; Service and Witness.*

- ### GREAT EVENTS, DEEP MEANINGS

  with the Revd Dr John Polkinghorne, Gordon Wilson, David Konstant – RC Bishop of Leeds, Fiona Castle, Dame Cicely Saunders and the Archbishop of York.

Tape	£7.00 (£6.00 each for 5 or more)
Photocopyable notes	£2.00

  SIX SESSIONS: *Christmas; Ash Wednesday; Palm Sunday; Good Friday; Easter; Pentecost.*

- ### THE TEACHING OF JESUS

  with the Revd Steve Chalke, Professor James Dunn, Dr Pauline Webb and the Archbishop of York.

Tape	£7.00 (£6.00 each for 5 or more)
Photocopyable notes	£2.00

  FIVE SESSIONS: *Forgiveness; God; Money; Heaven and Hell; On Being Human.*

- ### ATTENDING, EXPLORING, ENGAGING

  with the Archbishop of York, the Revd Steve Chalke, Fr Gerard Hughes SJ and Professor Frances Young

Tape	£7.50 (£6.50 each for 5 or more)
Photocopyable notes	£2.00

  FIVE SESSIONS: *Attending to God; Attending to One Another; Exploring Our Faith; Engaging with the World in Service; Engaging with the World in Evangelism.*

- **JESUS REDISCOVERED**

  with Paul Boateng MP, Dr Lavinia Byrne, the Revd Joel Edwards, the Revd Dr Tom Wright and the Archbishop of York.

Tape	£8.50 (£6.50 each for 5 or more.
Booklet	£2.75 (£1.75 each for 5 or more.

  FIVE SESSIONS: *Jesus' Life and Teaching; Following Jesus; Jesus: Saviour of the World; Jesus is Lord; Jesus and the Church.*

- **FAITH IN THE FIRE**

  with the Archbishop of York, Rabbi Lionel Blue, Steve Chalke, Dr Leslie Griffiths and Ann Widdecombe MP.

Tape	£8.50 (£6.50 each for 5 or more.
Booklet	£2.75 (£1.75 each for 5 or more.

  FIVE SESSIONS: *Faith facing Facts; Faith facing Doubt; Faith facing Disaster; Faith fuelling Prayer; Faith fuelling Action.*

- **IN THE WILDERNESS**

  with Cardinal Cormac Murphy-O'Connor, the Archbishop of York, the Revd Dr Rob Frost, the Revd Roy Jenkins and Dr Elaine Storkey.

Tape	£8.75 (£6.75 each for 5 or more.
Booklet	£2.95 (£1.95 each for 5 or more.

  FIVE SESSIONS: *Jesus, Satan and the Angels; The Wilderness Today; The Church in the Wilderness; Prayer, Meditation and Scripture; Solitude, Friendship and Fellowship.*

- **NEW WORLD, OLD FAITH**

  with Archbishop Rowan Williams, the Revd David Coffey, the Revd Joel Edwards, the Revd Dr John Polkinghorne and Dr Pauline Webb. Introduced by the Archbishop of York.

Tape	£8.95 (£6.95 each for 5 or more.
Booklet	£2.95 (£1.95 each for 5 or more.

  FIVE SESSIONS: *Brave New World?; Environmen and Ethics; Church and Family in Crisis?; One World - Many Faiths; Spirituality and Superstition.*

Also – TOPIC TAPES *for individual listening*

REDUCTIONS!
original price: £6.50

- **STRUGGLING/COPING**
  Tape 1: Living with depression,
           Living with panic attacks **£5.00**
  Tape 2: Living with cancer,
           Living with bereavement **£5.00**

- **SCIENCE AND CHRISTIAN FAITH** **£5.00**
  An in-depth discussion with the Revd Dr John Polkinghorne FRS KBE, former Professor of Mathematical Physics at Cambridge University.

- **EVANGELISM TODAY** **£5.00**
  with contributions by Canon Robin Gamble, the Revd Brian Hoare, Bishop Gavin Reid and Canon Robert Warren.

INEXPENSIVE-
designed as a 'give away'

FINDING FAITH is a twenty-minute audio tape, with four brief stories by people who have found faith, designed for enquirers and church members. It includes the Archbishop of York, comments by John Young and commentary by Simon Stanley. This tape was produced by York Courses for Churches Together in England.

£1.20 each   *10 or more* tapes – **95p each**

This tape accompanies the booklet entitled The Archbishop's School of Prayer.

PRAYER   **£3.50** *(£2.50 each for 5 or more)*
Side 1:   The Archbishop of York on Prayer
Side 2:   Four Christians on praying …
          for healing; in danger; in tongues;
          with perseverance.

IN PREPARATION

Christianity and Science – John Polkinghorne; *Healing and Wholeness* – John Wardle; *Life After Death* – David Winter

These booklets are commissioned by the Archbishop of York

THE ARCHBISHOP'S SCHOOL …
          … of Prayer … of the Sacraments
          … of Bible Reading … of Evangelism
Attractive yet inexpensive booklets for all.
          Single copy £1.25; 2-19 copies £1.10;
          20-49 copies 95p each; 50-99 copies 75p each;
          100 or more copies 62p each.
          SPECIAL OFFER *The Archbishop's School of Prayer* costs 75p (no limit on numbers) when ordered with at least one other item from these lists direct from York *Courses*.

York *Courses*

Books by John Young (author of the Course Booklets) available from York Courses

(All published by Hodder & Stoughton. Prices correct in December 2002)

• • •

TEACH YOURSELF CHRISTIANITY

An introduction to Christianity as a living faith; from Transubstantiation to the Toronto Blessing!

"not only informs, it excites" Dr David Hope, Archbishop of York

"… this important book" James Jones, Bishop of Liverpool

"An amazing compilation" Dr Peter Brierley   £8.99

• • •

WRESTLING WITH GIANTS

Stories by those who live with bereavement, depression, cancer, panic attacks and disability.

A valuable pastoral book for giving or lending.   £4.99

• • •

THE CASE AGAINST CHRIST

John Young acts as Counsel for the Defence in the Case against Christ.

"A classic" – CPAS

"… a remarkable achievement…" Lord Blanch

"Quite first class" Bishop Hugh Montefiore

"Does much to set the record straight" Sir Cliff Richard   £5.99

• • •

KNOW YOUR FAITH

A book for groups and individuals based on the great themes of the Christian faith as set out in the Apostles' Creed.

"A major resource" Dr George Carey, former Archbishop of Canterbury

"… rare freshness and vigour" Peter Forster, Bishop of Chester

"An excellent course" Revd Brian Hoare   · £4.99

We regret that we cannot accept card payments

If you wish to order any items from these lists, please send a cheque made out to York *Courses* to:

York Courses, PO Box 343, York YO19 5YB
Tel and Fax 01904 481677
email: admin@yorkcourses.clara.co.uk

ALL PRICES INCLUDE PACKING & SECOND CLASS POSTAGE IN THE UK

cause the massive rift in the Church of England which some predicted. Perhaps women bishops or the question of homosexual clergy will do just that. And, of course, the celibacy of the priesthood is a pressing issue for Roman Catholics. Large numbers of good clergy leave active ministry in order to marry – a great problem at a time when the supply of priests is drying up.

In May 2002 the Roman Catholic Archbishop of Sydney defended his policy of refusing to give the sacrament of holy communion to those wearing a rainbow sash to proclaim that they are practising homosexuals. He added, 'God made Adam and Eve, not Adam and Steve.' In contrast, some Bishops in the Anglican Communion bless same sex 'marriages' and Archbishop Rowan Williams has ordained a male priest who has a male partner.

The Christian family has changed over the years. There is less emphasis on family prayers or regular church attendance. Fewer children are well grounded in the Bible stories. Or so it seems to me. But I may be viewing the past through rose-coloured spectacles.

Sunday is less well observed as 'the Sabbath' than in the middle decades of the twentieth century. But I cannot feel deep sorrow for the passing of the Sundays of my childhood, when the whole world (the churches excepted) seemed to sleep. Today, Sunday trading, family outings and football leagues for young people are forcing the churches to rethink their programmes. Some are making imaginative use of the remaining six days.

One sad – indeed critical – feature of today's churches in Britain is the decline in numbers of young people. Two-thirds of the children of my generation attended Sunday-school. Today the churches are in contact with about 12% of the nation's young people.

Christian young people can have a tough time at school. I recall taking a Holy Communion service at our local church comprehensive school. At the invitation to come forward to receive the bread and wine, no one moved. After a painful silence, one girl stepped forward – rather red in the face, but determined. That act of witness was very costly for her but it encouraged others to follow.

Few things are more important than our prayers for Christian young people in school, at college, and at leisure. The secular pressures upon them are very strong.

The first recorded use of the word 'teenager' was in 1941 in an American scientific journal. The word was picked up in the 1950s by advertisers. Teenagers don't exist in the Bible, but the Scriptures are full of young people. Between 4,000 and 7,000 salaried youth workers are employed by the churches in Britain today. (Source: Peter Brierley of *Christian Research* and Steve Tilley)

Whether to take drugs, to experiment with sex or to leave the ('uncool') church – these are big questions for many teenagers from Christian homes, and peer pressure is sometimes difficult to resist.

Yet the Christian faith continues to flourish. The world Church grows by over 50,000 every day. The blood of the martyrs continues to be 'the seed of the church'. Dr David Barrett, a leading Church statistician, estimates that some 500 people die for their Christian faith every day in today's world.

Even in secular Britain, the local church can become the centre of a community in times of distress, as it did in Soham in 2002, following the murder of two young girls.

Many find that the old faith speaks to them in our new world, for it deals with the 'constants' in human nature. The cultural trappings may have changed since Bible times, but the underlying realities have not.

The Scriptures tell us about people who worked and worried, laughed and wept, struggled and survived, fell in and out of love, experienced loyalty and betrayal, grew sick and died. The Bible deals with these issues profoundly and helps us to set our lives within the love of God.

Everything has changed. And yet nothing has changed.

QUESTIONS FOR GROUPS

SUGGESTED BIBLE READING: Ephesians 4:22-32

1. Raise any points from this booklet or the audio tape with which you strongly agree or disagree.

2. On the tape, Joel Edwards and Rowan Williams suggest that credibility is a problem for today's Church. Do you agree? How can we tackle this?

3. (a) Do you value the greater informality and general modernisation of church worship? Or have we lost something important? What further changes (if any) would you like to see in your local church and in the wider Church?

   (b) In the light of today's secular Sunday, should churches modify their Sunday programmes and make better use of weekdays? If so, how?

4. Has there been a decline in the piety of the Christian family? Do you agree with Archbishop Rowan Williams and Dr Pauline Webb on the audio tape about grace at meals and 'the liturgy of the home'? Do we neglect the nurture of Christian children – surrendering too readily to secular values? How can we improve on this in a world where TV and peer pressure are so influential?

5. (a) Does today's divorce rate suggest a greater honesty within marriages, or do today's couples give up too easily?

    (b) Did the apparently stable family life of the first half of the last century hide deep unhappiness and abuse?

    (c) Should we allow remarriage in church? Is this question, together with gay issues and female bishops, likely to split the Church?

6. Christians spend much more time at work and at home than in church. Read John Robinson's words (see box) and consider how the churches can help their members to bear witness to their faith at work and in the home.

7. Christian young people can have a tough time. What are the pressures upon them and how can we support and encourage them? Can you give specific examples?

8. (a) Ideally, the local church is 'a family' with a mixture of ages. Is this true of your church? Should young people adapt to the older generation or vice versa? What might this mean in practice?

    (b) Today, many more homes are occupied by just one person. What does this mean in practical terms for the concept of church as family?

9. 'The Bible deals with the constants in human life'. Does the faith need reformulating to engage with the modern world? Or do the old orthodoxies (e.g. virgin birth, bodily resurrection, salvation through Christ, renewal by the Holy Spirit) still speak today, as Rowan Williams maintains?

10. Read Colossians 3:12-17 How can we apply this to the issues in this chapter? Does this mean that vigorous discussion – even conflict – within the Church (and within local churches) is always wrong?

'The laity are not the helpers of the clergy, so that they can do their job. The clergy are the helpers of the laity so that they can be the Church in the world.'

(Bishop John Robinson)

SESSION 4:
ONE WORLD – MANY FAITHS

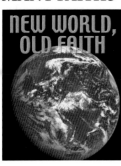

When I was a child, Britain was a 'Christian country'. Not everyone was an active church member, but most people regarded themselves as 'belonging' to one church or another. If you said that someone was not a Christian, this would usually be regarded as an insult. I recall someone saying rather aggressively, 'My brother is an atheist and a Communist but he's as good a Christian as you'! In some ways this was encouraging. He wanted to say that his brother was a good person, so he used the word 'Christian'.

Some of this lingers, but today more people want to use the word 'Christian' in its New Testament sense. Properly used, it is a *description* not a *compliment*. It describes someone who follows Jesus Christ – however inadequately – not just a 'nice' person.

How things can change in a couple of generations! In Britain we now have sizeable communities which live by other creeds. A senior member of the Royal Family recently made official visits to a Jain temple and a Zoroastrian community in Britain. Mosques and temples can be found in many towns along with churches and synagogues. In many other countries this has been the case for centuries of course. Now this situation is not 'over there' but over here as well.

What follows are a few direct and pithy statements arising from this situation. You may agree or disagree with them, but they should generate lively discussion.

In the modern world:
- 33% call themselves Christian
- 20% call themselves Muslim
- 13.5% call themselves Hindu
- 6% call themselves Buddhist
- 0.2% call themselves Jewish

These statistics, are taken from *Teach Yourself Christianity* by John Young, author of this course booklet.

- People of non-Christian faiths are still a small minority in Britain – no more than about 7%. Of these, most are Muslims but we also have Buddhists, Hindus, Jews, Sikhs, members of the Baha'i community and others.

- We should not lump all these communities together. There are considerable differences between them. In some cases this amounts to mutual hostility.

- We should judge other faiths by their best practices and highest ideals. Every faith community has its dark side. We would protest if others condemned Christianity because of Catholic/Protestant aggression in Northern Ireland.

- Every faith has its 'cultural' members as well as its committed members. This includes Christianity. I recall a man from Northern Ireland saying, 'I am an agnostic. But I am a *Protestant* agnostic'!

- We are called to take – and perhaps make – opportunities for discussion, friendship and mutual sharing with those of other faiths.

- There are no 'no go' areas for the gospel of Jesus Christ. We are called to respect others and to listen with courtesy. But we are also called to 'give a reason for the hope that is in us' (1 Peter 3:15). To withhold the gospel for fear of causing division is a form of unacceptable paternalism. Needless to say, we must share our faith with sensitivity and integrity.

- We cannot avoid the fact that the New Testament clearly teaches the uniqueness of Jesus Christ. 'Jesus is Lord' is the earliest Christian creed. Ever since Thomas acknowledged the risen Christ as 'my Lord and my God', Christians have worshipped him. This is unacceptable – even blasphemous – to some other faiths, but it is not negotiable by Christians.

- Some faiths and cultures are less worthy of respect than others. Some faiths (like neo-paganism and witchcraft) are deeply hostile to Christianity. Some cultures encourage harmful practices, e.g. forced marriages and female genital mutilation. In multi-cultural Britain it is tempting to fudge or ignore such issues, but they must be faced and resolved.

- Multi-faith worship can be an over-simple way of relating to other faiths. This sometimes means that anything distinctive to any one faith is screened out (e.g. praying to the Father through Jesus Christ). But sometimes multi-faith worship is essential – during great national celebrations for example, or to mark disasters which affect several faith communities. Shared silence can be one powerful ingredient on such occasions.

- We will find members of all the world faiths in heaven. They will be there, not because they are saved by their prophets, teachers or gurus, but because Jesus Christ has defeated death and thrown wide open the gates of glory. He – and only he – is 'the resurrection and the life' (John 11:25; see also Matthew 25:37-46).

- Fundamentalism has a bad name – understandably so, for fundamentalists of all faiths have committed terrible, sometimes violent, acts. But not all fundamentalists are extremists. Many are good citizens with a strong commitment and sincere (albeit over-simple) faith. They should not be vilified and used as scapegoats.

An Irula woman listens to a Scripture cassette. Photo: United Bible Societies

SUGGESTED BIBLE READING: John 4:1-14

1. Raise any points from this booklet or the audio tape with which you strongly agree or disagree.

2. (a) Do you have personal experience – direct or indirect – of people of other faiths?

   (b) Would you take part in multi-faith worship? Under what circumstances?

3. Should Christians evangelise people of other faiths, or is it best to 'live and let live'? Why?

4. (a) Read Hebrews 13:1-3
   Imagine that you are an elderly refugee or asylum seeker: exhausted, hungry and penniless. Should Britain be more welcoming? Should the churches take a stronger lead?

   (b) Is the Home Secretary right to want immigrants to learn English and to take part in a loyalty ceremony?

5. Recent research suggests that most people feel that Britain is a racist country, though less so than 10 years ago. One academic argues that racism is 'wired into' human beings, i.e. a tendency to think that 'our ways' are best. What do you make of all this?

6. (a) Is fundamentalism always as bad as it's painted? Do Christian fundamentalists have something to teach the rest of the Church?

   (b) Have September 11th 2001 and other atrocities destroyed our understanding of, and respect for, Islam and Muslims? If so, is this unfair – and dangerous?

7. Devoted members of other faiths challenge our own commitment. What can we learn from them?

8. In the Bible the word 'Christian' is a description not a compliment. How would you define 'Christian'? (After discussion, refer to the two definitions in the margins.)

9. A Muslim woman asks you to explain Christianity to her. How would you reply?

10. 'I am the way, the truth and the life. No one comes to the Father except through me'. (John 14:6; see also Acts 4:12). What are we to make of these statements in today's multi-faith world? Do you believe that people of all faiths will be found in heaven? Why?

'Being Christian means ... being people in whom his (Jesus') life and character and power are manifest and energised ... Christian experience is not so much a matter of imitating a leader ... as accepting and receiving a new quality of life – a life infinitely more profound and dynamic and meaningful than human life without Christ'

(Harry Williams)

SESSION 5:
SPIRITUALITY AND SUPERSTITION

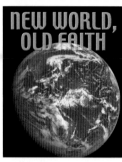
NEW WORLD, OLD FAITH

In Britain, more people attend churches than professional football matches. Characteristics of growing churches in Britain are included in *The Archbishop's School of Evangelism* (see blue centre pages).

There are more Anglicans in Africa than in all other continents put together.

According to some newspapers the Church is all but dead and buried. Such reports are greatly exaggerated but it is true that British church attendance figures have been in decline for many decades – a tendency shared with all other Western European countries.

To get a true perspective, we need to note several other factors.

- The world Church is growing (see Session 3). Christianity remains the largest movement ever, easily outstripping other world faiths. I report this, not in a spirit of triumphalism, but simply as a significant fact.

- Many churches in Britain are growing. Common characteristics of growing churches have been the subject of research and are readily available.

- Largely as a result of the missionary expansion of the 18th and 19th centuries, the centre of gravity of Christendom has now shifted from those countries (including Britain) which sent missionaries, to nations in Africa, Asia and Latin America.

- The majority of Christians in today's world are not white, grey-haired and affluent (though there are still a lot of us about!) but black, poor, Pentecostal and young. There is hope for the future!

- Spirituality is thriving. It must be tough to be a zealous card-carrying atheist in Britain today. For the decline in religious practice has not resulted in a generation of atheists. Interest in spirituality is growing in so-called 'secular' Britain and most people believe in God, prayer and angels.

It was G. K. Chesterton who observed that when people stop believing in God, they don't believe in nothing – they believe in *anything*. There are some zany ideas out there! And there is a great deal of confusion. David Beckham illustrated this when he said that he wanted his son Brooklyn to be christened but admitted that he was unsure about which religion he should be christened into.

In 1959 the philosopher Alasdair MacIntyre observed that no one believes in astrology. If that was true then, it certainly isn't true today. Horoscopes are found in most newspapers. Many people take them at least half seriously and some people base important decisions upon them. Many footballers famously – and without embarrassment – go through a series of complicated rituals designed to bring good luck on the pitch. Most towns have a thriving 'New Age' bookshop and some non-Christians devote a challenging amount of time to meditation and to the practice and exploration of their beliefs.

Dr David Hay's research shows that a large and growing number in modern Britain claim to have had a 'spiritual experience' – though different people understand different things by that phrase. Best known are 'near-death' experiences. A friend who is an ambulance driver told me how he and his colleagues vigorously pounded a woman's chest to re-activate her heart. They were successful and later he was able to ask her about that experience. She did not talk about the pain of being pummelled but about a beautiful experience of warmth, light and peace. This is a typical description of a 'near-death experience', as is the disappearance of any fear of death.

Many people in modern Britain would describe themselves as 'spiritual' but not necessarily 'religious'. The term *spirituality* embraces a wide range of activities – from hugging trees and casting spells to meditation and prayer. In view of this breadth it is important to ask of any spirituality:

- is it challenging as well as encouraging?
- is it life-enhancing?
- does it show concern for other people and for the environment?
- is it centred on God or on self-awareness?
- does it provide a resource for living in the 21st century?

Perhaps the stress on spirituality in today's world will encourage Christians to re-engage seriously with the foundation stones of their own faith: prayer, worship, Bible reading and fellowship.

Modern Britain resembles ancient Athens (Acts 17) – plus mobile phones and parking problems of course! Does this present an opportunity for the gospel? Clearly it does, but only if modern Christians and the churches to which they belong, are prepared to engage with our secular and superstitious culture with energy, imagination and sensitivity.

Over to you. And over to me.

QUESTIONS FOR GROUPS

SUGGESTED BIBLE READING: Luke 11:1-13

Quakers believe that the Inner Light is a great gift from God. Others, e.g. the philosopher Alasdair MacIntyre, maintain that it is the worst kind of lighting because it is dangerously subjective.

1. Raise any points from this booklet or the audio tape with which you strongly agree or disagree.

2. Each of our participants has had a spiritual experience. What do you understand by that term? Have you had one – or many? Can such experiences be misleading as well as enlightening, making us prey to wishful thinking or irrational urges, as Joel Edwards suggests?

3. What do you make of 'near-death experiences'?

4. 'Our world is a mixture of the secular, the superstitious and the spiritual'. Is this true? If so, what opportunities and challenges does this present for the gospel? How can the churches (nationally and locally) engage with the prevalent 'pick-and-mix' approach to faith?

5. How strongly do you personally feel the pull of secularism and superstition? Have they invaded the Church?

6. (a) How would you defend Christianity against the charge that it is nothing more than a complicated superstition?

   (b) Should a Christian practise superstitions and read horoscopes, or are these a denial of the faith?

7. Non-Christian meditation seeks to put us in touch with our 'inner self'. Christian meditation seeks to put us in touch with the Living God. Is this a fair distinction?

8. (a) Research suggests that prayer, meditation and worship are good for our health. What do you make of this?

   (b) 'Too few Christians have learned to pray.' True or false? If true, what can we do about it? Share your personal experience of prayer.

Twenty years ago, I was driving up the M1 to Sheffield, on All Souls' night. It was the year after my mother died and *Messiah* was playing full blast on the car radio. Just for a moment, I had the certainty of resurrection. (The novelist Margaret Drabble)

9. (a) Many commentators sense a 'spiritual hunger' in the modern world. What can the Church (nationally and locally) do to meet this need?

   (b) Rather embarrassed, a friend says 'You go to church. Can you teach me to pray?' How would you respond?

10. Read Acts 17:16-34 What similarities and differences strike you about Paul's world and ours? What can we learn from his approach to the Athenians?